The Heist Against Society

I0406950

By Harry Holland

TABLE OF CONTENTS

CHAPTER 1: EMBRACING YOUR UNIQUENESS

In a world that often demands conformity and adherence to societal norms, it takes courage to break away and embrace your uniqueness. You, dear reader, are a black sheep—a maverick among the herd, and this chapter is dedicated to helping you recognize the power and potential that lies within your nonconformity.

Societal norms can be suffocating. They dictate what we should wear, how we should behave, and even the dreams we should pursue. But what if I told you that being the black sheep is a gift? It is an opportunity to carve your own path, to challenge the status quo, and to create a life that aligns with your authentic self.

When you embrace your uniqueness, you set yourself apart from the crowd. You become a beacon of individuality, shining a light on the possibilities that lie beyond the well-trodden path. But this journey is not without its challenges. Breaking away from societal norms can invite judgment and criticism from those who are uncomfortable with your audacity.

To navigate this path, you must develop resilience. Understand that the judgments of others are often a reflection of their own insecurities and limitations. Embrace the audacity within you—the audacity to be different, to defy expectations, and to pursue your own version of success. The world needs more mavericks who are willing to challenge the norm and forge new paths.

But embracing your uniqueness goes beyond defying societal expectations. It's about discovering and embracing your true self. Take the time to explore your passions, interests, and values. What sets your soul on fire? What makes you come alive? Embrace those passions wholeheartedly, even if they deviate from the expectations of others.

Embracing your uniqueness also means giving yourself permission to fail. It means stepping outside of your comfort zone, even when it feels uncomfortable or uncertain. Remember, the black sheep is not afraid to stumble or make mistakes. Instead, they view setbacks as opportunities for growth and learning.

Practical Point: Take some time to reflect on your own uniqueness. What are your passions, interests, and values? How can you incorporate more of these elements into your life? Start by making a list of the things that make you different and unique. Embrace them fully and use them as a foundation for building a life that aligns with your authentic self.

As you embark on this journey of embracing your uniqueness, surround yourself with a supportive community. Seek out like-minded individuals who share your vision and values. Connect with fellow black sheep who are also challenging societal norms and pursuing unconventional paths. Together, you can provide each other with encouragement, inspiration, and the strength to persevere in the face of criticism.

Remember, you are not alone. There is an entire tribe of black sheep out there, ready to welcome you with open arms. Embrace your uniqueness, and let it propel you forward on the path to personal and professional fulfillment.

CHAPTER 2: THE MAVERICK MINDSET

In a world that often promotes conformity and mediocrity, cultivating a maverick mindset is essential to thrive outside the box. It is about embracing audacity, boldness, and cheekiness as you challenge the status quo and forge your own path to success. In this chapter, we will explore practical strategies to develop a maverick mindset and unleash your creativity and innovation.

Embracing audacity is the first step towards breaking free from societal limitations. It's about having the courage to question the norms and expectations that have been imposed upon you. The maverick refuses to accept the boundaries others set and instead pushes the limits of what is possible. It requires stepping outside your comfort zone, taking calculated risks, and embracing failure as an opportunity for growth.

To develop audacity, start by identifying areas in your life where you've been playing it safe. Are there dreams you've put on hold? Are there risks you've been afraid to take? Make a list of these areas and challenge yourself to take bold action. Whether it's pursuing a new career path, starting a business, or expressing yourself creatively, audacity is about pushing through fear and taking action despite uncertainty.

Boldness is another key trait of the maverick mindset. It involves being unapologetically yourself and standing up for what you believe in. Boldness is about daring to be different, even when it feels uncomfortable or unpopular. It requires authenticity, integrity, and a willingness to go against the grain.

To cultivate boldness, start by embracing your uniqueness and celebrating your individuality. Identify your core values and principles, and let them guide your actions and decisions. Speak your truth, even when it challenges the status quo. Surround yourself with supportive individuals who encourage your authenticity and inspire you to be bold.

Cheekiness is the third pillar of the maverick mindset. It is the ability to challenge authority, conventional wisdom, and the limitations others place upon you. Cheekiness is about playfully bending the rules, finding creative solutions, and thinking outside the box. It encourages innovation and allows you to discover unconventional paths to success.

To develop cheekiness, start by questioning the assumptions and beliefs that society has ingrained in you. Challenge the "shoulds" and "musts" that dictate your actions. Look for opportunities to approach problems from a fresh perspective, asking yourself, "How can I do this differently?" Embrace experimentation and curiosity as you explore new ways of thinking and problem-solving.

Cultivating a maverick mindset also requires fostering an environment that nurtures creativity and innovation. Surround yourself with diverse perspectives and seek out new experiences that broaden your horizons. Embrace lifelong learning and continuous personal growth. Stay open-minded and curious, and be willing to adapt and evolve as you navigate the ever-changing landscape of life and work.

Practical Points:

Identify one area in your life where you have been playing it safe. Take a bold step towards breaking free from that limitation.

Challenge one assumption or belief that society has imposed upon you. Question its validity and explore alternative perspectives.

Surround yourself with individuals who inspire audacity, boldness, and cheekiness. Seek out role models and mentors who embody the maverick mindset.

Create a creative space or routine that encourages innovation. Dedicate time each day to exploring new ideas and thinking outside the box.

Embrace failure as a learning opportunity. Shift your perspective and view setbacks as stepping stones to success.

By embracing audacity, boldness, and cheekiness, you are priming your mind for innovation, creativity, and success. The maverick mindset will enable you to navigate the challenges of carving your own path and create a life and career that aligns with your authentic self.

CHAPTER 3: PLAYING BY YOUR OWN RULES

In a world filled with societal norms and expectations, daring to challenge them is a radical act of self-empowerment. This chapter is an invitation to break free from the chains of conformity and embrace non-traditional approaches to life and work. By defying conventional wisdom, you can forge a path that aligns with your values, passions, and vision of success.

Challenging traditional norms and expectations requires a deep understanding of your own desires and a willingness to listen to your inner voice. It starts by questioning the beliefs and assumptions that society imposes upon you. Ask yourself, "Why should I follow this path? What are the alternatives?" Dig deep into your values and aspirations, and dare to choose a different route.

Embracing non-traditional approaches to life and work opens up a world of possibilities. It means being open to unconventional career paths, alternative lifestyles, and unique ways of achieving success. It's about exploring new avenues and creating your own definition of what it means to thrive.

To embrace non-traditional approaches, start by identifying the areas of your life where you feel the strongest pull toward breaking free from convention. Is it in your career, relationships, or lifestyle choices? Reflect on what truly matters to you and consider how you can align your choices with your values. Give yourself permission to think outside the box and explore uncharted territory.

Finding success on your own terms requires redefining what success means to you. It's about moving away from society's narrow definition of achievement and creating a personalized metric for fulfillment. Success can be measured in terms of personal growth, impact on others, or the alignment between your work and passions. Explore what success looks like to you and set goals that reflect your unique definition.

Practical Points:

Identify one area of your life where you feel the strongest urge to challenge traditional norms and expectations. Consider how you can take a step toward defying convention in that area.

Question the beliefs and assumptions that society has ingrained in you. Take time to reflect on why you've been following certain paths and whether there are alternative approaches that resonate more with your authentic self.

Explore non-traditional career paths or ways of working that align with your passions and values. Research alternative industries, unconventional job roles, or opportunities for entrepreneurship that excite you.

Embrace experimentation and adaptability. Allow yourself to take risks and learn from failures along the way. Remember that non-traditional approaches often involve exploring uncharted territory, and that can come with its own set of challenges and rewards.

Surround yourself with a supportive community. Seek out individuals who have defied convention and achieved success on their own terms. Engage in conversations, join communities, and cultivate relationships that encourage and inspire your non-traditional journey.

By challenging traditional norms and embracing non-traditional approaches, you open up a world of possibilities. You free yourself from the constraints of societal expectations and create a life that is uniquely yours.

CHAPTER 4: REMOTE WORKING

The rise of remote work has revolutionized the way we approach our careers and lifestyles. In this chapter, we will explore the benefits and challenges of remote work, as well as provide practical strategies for creating a productive remote work routine. Additionally, we will discuss how to harness technology to enhance flexibility and freedom in your work and personal life.

Remote work offers a plethora of benefits that can transform your work-life balance. Firstly, it provides the opportunity to work from anywhere, giving you the freedom to choose your ideal work environment. Whether it's a cozy home office, a vibrant coffee shop, or a beautiful beachside location, remote work allows you to design your surroundings to optimize productivity and inspiration.

Furthermore, remote work liberates you from the constraints of traditional office hours. Instead of adhering to a rigid 9-to-5 schedule, remote work allows you to create a flexible routine that aligns with your natural energy levels and personal commitments. You can structure your workday to accommodate personal interests, family responsibilities, or even pursue other passions alongside your career.

However, remote work does present unique challenges that require conscious effort to overcome. The freedom and flexibility it offers can blur the boundaries between work and personal life, making it crucial to establish clear boundaries and routines. Without structure, remote work can lead to burnout or inefficiency. It's important to find a balance that allows you to be productive while also maintaining a healthy work-life integration.

Creating a productive remote work routine begins with understanding your individual needs and preferences. Consider your most productive hours, your preferred working environment, and the tools and resources that enable your best work. Experiment with different approaches until you find a routine that optimizes your performance and well-being.

To enhance your remote work experience, technology becomes an invaluable ally. Take advantage of various digital tools and platforms that facilitate collaboration, communication, and task management. Virtual meetings, project management software, and cloud-based document sharing enable seamless collaboration with colleagues and clients, regardless of geographical distances.

Practical Points:

Designate a dedicated workspace that is conducive to focus and productivity. Create a physical environment that inspires and energizes you, whether it's a separate room or a designated corner in your home.

Establish a consistent routine that aligns with your natural energy levels and personal commitments. Determine your most productive hours and structure your work accordingly. Set boundaries around your work time to ensure a healthy work-life balance.

Embrace technology to enhance your remote work experience. Explore digital tools and platforms that can streamline your workflow, facilitate communication, and improve collaboration with colleagues and clients.

Prioritize self-discipline and time management. Set clear goals and deadlines for your work and hold yourself accountable. Establish regular check-ins to track progress and adjust your approach if needed.

Seek opportunities for social connection and community engagement. Remote work can sometimes feel isolating, so make an effort to connect with colleagues, join virtual professional communities, or participate in networking events to foster meaningful relationships.

Remote work has the potential to revolutionize your work-life balance, providing you with the freedom and flexibility to design a fulfilling career and lifestyle. By creating a productive remote work routine and harnessing the power of technology, you can thrive in a remote work environment and enjoy the benefits it offers.

CHAPTER 5: EXPANDING YOUR HORIZONS

Human connections and experiences shape our lives in profound ways. In this chapter, we will explore the concept of non-monogamy, not only in the realm of relationships but also in our approach to life. We will discuss the joys and challenges of embracing diverse relationships and connections, as well as the transformative power of travel and exploration.

Embracing diverse relationships and connections is a fundamental aspect of personal growth and expanding our horizons. By breaking free from societal expectations and embracing non-monogamy, we open ourselves to a world of new possibilities. Non-monogamy allows for deeper connections with multiple individuals, fostering a sense of intimacy, understanding, and personal development that is often limited in traditional monogamous relationships.

However, non-monogamy requires a thoughtful and ethical approach. It is important to communicate openly and honestly with all parties involved, ensuring that everyone's boundaries, needs, and desires are respected. Non-monogamy invites us to challenge traditional notions of possessiveness and exclusivity, creating space for diverse relationship structures such as polyamory, open relationships, or other forms of consensual non-monogamy.

Non-monogamy also extends beyond relationships to encompass a broader mindset of exploration and curiosity. Just as we embrace diverse connections with people, we can also cultivate a non-monogamous approach to places. The transformative power of travel and exploration allows us to break free from our comfort zones, immerse ourselves in new cultures, and broaden our perspectives.

Travel opens our eyes to the vastness of the world and the richness of human experiences. It challenges our preconceived notions and invites us to question our own beliefs and biases. Through travel, we gain a deeper understanding of different cultures, traditions, and ways of life. We learn to appreciate diversity and celebrate the beauty of our shared humanity.

Practical Points:

Embrace diverse relationships: Reflect on your values and desires, and explore relationship models beyond traditional monogamy. Engage in open and honest communication with your partners to ensure everyone's needs and boundaries are respected.

Cultivate a spirit of exploration: Embrace the transformative power of travel. Plan trips to new destinations, both near and far, and immerse yourself in different cultures. Engage with locals, try new activities, and step out of your comfort zone to broaden your perspective.

Practice cultural sensitivity and empathy: Respect the customs and traditions of the places you visit. Seek to understand and appreciate cultural differences, and approach new experiences with an open mind and heart. Be mindful of your impact as a visitor and strive to leave a positive impression.

Foster meaningful connections: While traveling, engage with locals and fellow travelers to forge authentic connections. Embrace the opportunity to learn from different perspectives and engage in meaningful conversations. Be open to forming friendships that transcend borders and cultures.

Embrace a non-monogamous mindset in life: Extend the principles of non-monogamy beyond relationships and apply them to various aspects of your life. Challenge conventional beliefs, seek diverse experiences, and explore different paths to personal growth and fulfillment.

By embracing diverse relationships and connections and adopting a non-monogamous mindset, both in relationships and in life, we open ourselves up to a world of possibilities. We enrich our lives with deeper connections, cultural experiences, and personal growth. Embrace the transformative power of non-monogamy with people and places, and watch as your horizons expand and your understanding of the world deepens.

CHAPTER 6: LIFE IS SHORT

Life is a precious and fleeting gift, and it is up to us to make the most of every moment. In this chapter, we will explore the concept of seizing opportunities with gusto, overcoming fear, and taking calculated risks in pursuit of our dreams. We will delve into the mindset and strategies necessary to embrace a sense of urgency and make the most of the time we have.

Embracing a sense of urgency in pursuing your dreams is essential because time waits for no one. Often, we find ourselves stuck in the comfort of our routines, hesitating to step outside our comfort zones. However, it is when we challenge ourselves, take risks, and embrace new experiences that we truly grow and thrive.

Overcoming fear is a crucial step in seizing opportunities. Fear often holds us back from pursuing our dreams and reaching our full potential. However, it is important to remember that fear is a natural response to the unknown. By acknowledging our fears and understanding that they do not define us, we can move past them and take bold action.

Taking calculated risks involves weighing the potential rewards against the potential consequences. It requires careful consideration and planning, but it also means being willing to step into the unknown. Risks can lead to significant personal and professional growth, as well as unexpected opportunities and achievements.

Carpe diem, the Latin phrase meaning "seize the day," encapsulates the essence of living life to the fullest. It reminds us to make the most of each moment and to not postpone our dreams and aspirations. By embracing the philosophy of carpe diem, we open ourselves to a world of possibilities and create a life filled with purpose and fulfillment.

Practical Points:

Identify your dreams and goals: Take time to reflect on what truly matters to you. Identify your dreams, passions, and goals, both personally and professionally. Clarify what you want to achieve and what brings you joy and fulfillment.

Break down your goals into actionable steps: Once you have identified your dreams and goals, break them down into smaller, actionable steps. This will help you create a roadmap to success and make your aspirations feel more attainable.

Embrace discomfort and challenge: Growth often happens outside of our comfort zones. Embrace discomfort and be willing to challenge yourself. Take on new experiences, learn new skills, and push your boundaries. Embracing discomfort will expand your capabilities and open doors to new opportunities.

Develop resilience and perseverance: Seizing opportunities with gusto requires resilience and perseverance. Understand that setbacks and obstacles are a natural part of the journey. Cultivate a mindset of resilience and view challenges as opportunities for growth. Develop strategies to bounce back from failures and setbacks, and never lose sight of your goals.

Surround yourself with support: Seek out a supportive community or network of individuals who believe in you and your dreams. Surround yourself with people who inspire and encourage you. Their support can provide motivation, guidance, and accountability as you pursue your goals.

Celebrate progress and small victories: Acknowledge and celebrate the progress you make along the way. Recognize and appreciate the small victories, as they contribute to your overall growth and success. Celebrating milestones boosts motivation and helps maintain momentum.

Remember, life is short, and each day is an opportunity to make a difference and create a life of meaning and fulfillment. Seize the day, overcome fear, and take calculated risks in pursuit of your dreams. Embrace a sense of urgency and live with gusto, making the most of every moment.

CHAPTER 7: HOLDING THE FRAME

Life is a journey filled with ups and downs, and along the way, we are bound to face setbacks and obstacles. In this chapter, we will explore the importance of building resilience to navigate through challenges, developing a positive mindset, and overcoming obstacles that come our way. By holding the frame and cultivating mental and emotional strength, we can rise above adversity and continue moving forward towards our goals and dreams.

Cultivating mental and emotional strength is essential in building resilience. It involves developing self-awareness, managing emotions, and maintaining a positive outlook in the face of adversity. By understanding our thoughts and emotions, we can gain control over our responses and choose empowering perspectives that fuel our resilience.

Developing a positive mindset is a powerful tool in overcoming setbacks and obstacles. It allows us to reframe challenges as opportunities for growth and learning. By focusing on solutions rather than dwelling on problems, we can develop a proactive approach to challenges and maintain our motivation and determination.

Overcoming setbacks and obstacles requires a strategic approach. It involves breaking down problems into manageable steps, seeking support and guidance when needed, and staying committed to our goals. By adopting a growth mindset, we can view setbacks as temporary hurdles and learn from them, which ultimately strengthens our resilience.

Practical Points:

Cultivate self-awareness: Take time to reflect on your thoughts, emotions, and reactions to challenges. Develop an understanding of how you respond to adversity and identify patterns or triggers that may hinder your resilience. This self-awareness will enable you to make conscious choices and develop strategies to overcome obstacles.

Practice reframing: When faced with setbacks or obstacles, consciously reframe them as opportunities for growth and learning. Reframing challenges allows you to maintain a positive mindset and see the potential for personal development and success. Look for the lessons and silver linings in every situation.

Develop problem-solving skills: Break down challenges into smaller, manageable steps. This approach allows you to tackle obstacles systematically and maintain a sense of progress. Seek creative solutions and explore different perspectives. Consider seeking advice or support from mentors or experts who can provide guidance and insights.

Build a support system: Surround yourself with a network of supportive individuals who believe in your potential and provide encouragement during challenging times. Seek out mentors or peers who have overcome similar obstacles and learn from their experiences. Their support can provide guidance, accountability, and motivation.

Practice self-care: Take care of your physical, mental, and emotional well-being. Engage in activities that recharge you and reduce stress, such as exercise, meditation, or spending time in nature. Prioritize self-care to maintain your resilience and prevent burnout during challenging times.

Embrace failure as a stepping stone to success: Failure is an inevitable part of life, but it is how we respond to failure that determines our resilience. Embrace failure as an opportunity for growth and learning. Analyze the lessons it offers and use them to improve and adapt your approach moving forward.

Celebrate small victories: Acknowledge and celebrate your progress, no matter how small. Recognize the effort and resilience you demonstrate along the way. Celebrating small victories boosts motivation and reinforces your belief in your ability to overcome challenges.

Remember, building resilience is a lifelong process. It requires consistent practice, self-reflection, and a commitment to personal growth. By holding the frame, cultivating mental and emotional strength, and developing a positive mindset, you can navigate through challenges with resilience and continue progressing towards your goals and dreams.

CHAPTER 8: FINANCES: ESCAPING THE DEBT TRAP

Financial freedom is a key aspect of living a liberated and fulfilling life. In this chapter, we will explore strategies for escaping the debt trap, prioritizing debt repayment, and embracing a lifestyle of living within your means. By taking control of your finances and eliminating debt, you can pave the way for greater financial security and freedom.

Prioritizing debt repayment is an important step towards financial freedom. It requires a shift in mindset and a commitment to taking action. By facing your debt head-on and creating a plan to pay it off, you can regain control over your financial situation. Prioritize your debt payments based on interest rates, starting with high-interest debts and working your way down. Consider utilizing strategies such as the snowball or avalanche method to accelerate your progress.

Strategies for eliminating debt and avoiding new ones are crucial for achieving long-term financial stability. Start by identifying the root causes of your debt and addressing them. This may involve adjusting your spending habits, creating a budget, and practicing mindful spending. Track your expenses and identify areas where you can cut back or find more affordable alternatives. Avoid taking on new debt unless it is absolutely necessary and consider saving up for purchases instead.

Living within your means is a powerful tool for financial freedom. It involves aligning your spending with your income and avoiding excessive or unnecessary expenses. By embracing a minimalist mindset and redefining success beyond material possessions, you can prioritize experiences and personal growth over accumulating things. Evaluate your needs versus wants and focus on what truly brings you fulfillment and joy. Practice gratitude for what you have and cultivate contentment in the present moment.

Practical Points:

Create a debt repayment plan: Take an inventory of your debts and create a plan to pay them off systematically. Prioritize high-interest debts and consider consolidation or refinancing options to reduce interest rates. Set specific goals and track your progress along the way.

Adjust your spending habits: Assess your spending patterns and identify areas where you can cut back or find more cost-effective alternatives. Create a realistic budget that aligns with your income and financial goals. Consider using budgeting tools or apps to track your expenses and hold yourself accountable.

Practice mindful spending: Before making a purchase, ask yourself if it aligns with your values and priorities. Consider the long-term impact of your spending decisions and opt for experiences and investments that contribute to your personal growth and well-being. Avoid impulse buying and give yourself time to reflect on purchases before making them.

Build an emergency fund: Set aside a portion of your income regularly to build an emergency fund. Aim to save at least three to six months' worth of living expenses. Having a financial safety net provides peace of mind and protects you from unexpected setbacks or emergencies.

Seek professional advice if needed: If you feel overwhelmed by your financial situation or unsure of how to proceed, consider seeking guidance from a financial advisor or a credit counselor. They can provide personalized advice and strategies based on your specific circumstances.

Cultivate a minimalist mindset: Embrace the philosophy of living with less and prioritizing experiences over material possessions. Practice gratitude for what you have and avoid the trap of constantly chasing after more. Focus on creating a life filled with meaning, purpose, and fulfillment.

Celebrate milestones: As you make progress in eliminating debt and living within your means, celebrate your milestones. Acknowledge the hard work and discipline it takes to achieve financial freedom. Reward yourself with experiences or small treats that align with your values and do not derail your progress.

Remember, escaping the debt trap and living within your means is a journey that requires commitment and perseverance. By prioritizing debt repayment, implementing strategies to avoid new debt, and embracing a minimalist mindset, you can regain control over your finances and pave the way for a life of financial freedom and abundance.

CHAPTER 9: THE FUCK IT FUND

Financial security is a crucial aspect of building a life of freedom and abundance. In this chapter, we will explore the concept of the "Fuck It Fund" and its role in creating a robust savings account or investment portfolio. By establishing this fund, you can weather financial storms with confidence and gain greater control over your financial future.

Building a robust savings account or investment portfolio is the foundation of financial security. It provides a safety net during uncertain times and empowers you to take calculated risks in pursuit of your dreams. Start by setting clear savings goals and creating a budget that allows you to allocate a portion of your income towards your Fuck It Fund. Aim to save at least three to six months' worth of living expenses as an initial target.

Strategies for automating savings and compounding wealth can help accelerate your progress towards financial security. Set up automatic transfers from your checking account to your savings or investment accounts. This ensures that a portion of your income is consistently being saved without requiring regular manual intervention. Additionally, consider taking advantage of compounding interest by investing in vehicles such as retirement accounts or low-cost index funds.

Weathering financial storms with confidence requires a combination of preparedness and resilience. Prepare for unexpected expenses by having adequate insurance coverage, such as health insurance, home insurance, and car insurance. Additionally, consider diversifying your income streams to reduce reliance on a single source of income. This could involve creating multiple streams of income, such as freelancing, side businesses, or passive income from investments.

Practical Points:

Set clear savings goals: Determine the amount you aim to save in your Fuck It Fund and break it down into achievable milestones. Make saving a priority and track your progress regularly. Celebrate each milestone along the way to stay motivated.

Create a budget: Develop a budget that aligns with your financial goals and allows you to save consistently. Identify areas where you can cut back on expenses and redirect those funds towards your savings. Consider using budgeting tools or apps to simplify the process.

Automate your savings: Set up automatic transfers from your checking account to your savings or investment accounts. This ensures that a portion of your income is consistently saved without requiring constant manual intervention. Treat your savings as a non-negotiable expense.

Explore investment options: Once you have built a solid savings foundation, consider exploring investment options that align with your risk tolerance and long-term goals. Consult with a financial advisor if needed to help you make informed investment decisions.

Prepare for emergencies: In addition to your Fuck It Fund, ensure you have adequate insurance coverage to protect yourself and your assets. Research and compare different insurance options to find the coverage that best suits your needs.

Diversify your income streams: Consider creating multiple streams of income to enhance your financial security. Explore opportunities for freelancing, side businesses, or investments that generate passive income. Diversifying your income reduces the risk associated with relying on a single source of income.

Maintain a frugal mindset: Practice mindful spending and resist the temptation to succumb to lifestyle inflation as your income increases. Continually evaluate your expenses and prioritize experiences and investments that align with your values and long-term goals.

Stay informed and adapt: Keep up with changes in the financial landscape and adapt your strategies accordingly. Continuously educate yourself about personal finance, investment trends, and economic developments. Being proactive and adaptable is key to maintaining financial security.

Establishing a Fuck It Fund empowers you to navigate financial challenges with greater ease and confidence. By building a robust savings account or investment portfolio, automating your savings, and diversifying your income streams, you can weather financial storms and create a solid foundation for your financial future.

CHAPTER 10: DEMYSTIFYING THE WORLD OF MONEY

Understanding the basics of investing and financial literacy is a crucial step towards achieving long-term financial growth and freedom. In this chapter, we will demystify the world of money and guide you through the fundamentals of investing. By developing a solid foundation of knowledge, you can navigate the investment landscape with simplicity and clarity.

Investing is the process of allocating money with the expectation of generating a return or profit over time. It involves putting your money to work in various assets such as stocks, bonds, real estate, or businesses. While investing can seem intimidating, especially if you're new to the concept, it is a powerful tool for building wealth and achieving your financial goals.

To begin, it's essential to understand the different investment options available to you. Stocks represent ownership in a company and offer the potential for capital appreciation and dividends. Bonds, on the other hand, are debt instruments where investors lend money to governments or corporations in exchange for regular interest payments and the return of the principal amount at maturity. Real estate investments involve purchasing properties or investing in real estate investment trusts (REITs) that generate income through rental or property value appreciation.

Navigating the investment landscape with simplicity and clarity requires a diversified approach. Diversification involves spreading your investments across different asset classes, industries, and geographic regions. This helps mitigate risk and maximize potential returns. By diversifying, you reduce the impact of any single investment on your overall portfolio, increasing its stability and resilience.

Long-term investment strategies are key to sustained wealth

growth. Investing is not a get-rich-quick scheme; it requires patience and consistency. A long-term perspective allows you to ride out market fluctuations and take advantage of compounding returns. Compounding is the process of earning returns on your initial investment and subsequent returns. Over time, compounding can significantly boost your investment gains.

Practical Points:

Educate yourself: Begin by reading books, articles, and reputable online resources that provide insights into investing and financial literacy. Understand key concepts such as risk and return, asset allocation, diversification, and the power of compounding.

Set financial goals: Clearly define your financial goals and time horizons. Are you investing for retirement, a down payment on a house, or your children's education? Establishing specific goals will guide your investment strategy and help you make informed decisions.

Determine your risk tolerance: Assess your risk tolerance by considering your financial situation, investment timeline, and comfort with volatility. Investments carry varying degrees of risk, and it's important to align your portfolio with your risk tolerance to ensure you can stay committed during market downturns.

Start with a diversified portfolio: Begin investing by constructing a diversified portfolio that includes a mix of stocks, bonds, and other asset classes. This helps spread risk and capture potential returns from different areas of the market.

Take advantage of tax-advantaged accounts: Explore tax-advantaged investment accounts such as individual retirement accounts (IRAs) or employer-sponsored retirement plans like 401(k)s. These accounts offer tax benefits that can enhance your long-term investment returns.

Invest regularly and automate contributions: Consistency is key in investing. Set up automatic contributions to your investment accounts, allowing you to regularly invest without needing to remember to do so manually. This helps you avoid emotional decision-making and ensures you stay on track with your investment plan.

Review and rebalance: Regularly review your portfolio to ensure it aligns with your financial goals and risk tolerance. Rebalance your portfolio periodically to maintain your desired asset allocation and adjust for any significant changes in market conditions.

Seek professional guidance if needed: Consider consulting with a financial advisor if you feel overwhelmed or unsure about your investment decisions. A qualified advisor can provide personalized guidance based on your unique circumstances and goals.

By understanding the basics of investing and finance, you can confidently navigate the world of money. Remember, investing is a long-term commitment that requires patience, consistency, and ongoing education. Stay informed, review your portfolio periodically, and make adjustments as needed to ensure your investments align with your goals and risk tolerance.

CHAPTER 11: IGNORING THE ILLUSION

In a world filled with promises of overnight success and get-rich-quick schemes, it is crucial to maintain a discerning eye and avoid falling into the trap of illusions. Building lasting wealth requires a mindset focused on patience, consistency, and a long-term perspective. In this chapter, we will explore the importance of identifying and avoiding financial scams and trends while emphasizing the value of building wealth through sustainable practices.

Educate Yourself: The first step in avoiding get-rich-quick schemes is to educate yourself about common financial scams and trends. Stay informed about the warning signs and red flags associated with fraudulent investment opportunities. Research and understand the principles behind legitimate wealth-building strategies. By arming yourself with knowledge, you can make informed decisions and protect your hard-earned money.

Be Skeptical of Unbelievable Claims: If an investment opportunity promises extraordinary returns with little to no risk or effort, exercise caution. Remember that if something sounds too good to be true, it probably is. Genuine wealth-building endeavors require time, effort, and calculated risk-taking. Avoid succumbing to the allure of quick riches and stay focused on sustainable, long-term financial growth.

Conduct Due Diligence: Before committing your money to any investment, conduct thorough due diligence. Research the investment opportunity, the company or individual offering it, and their track record. Look for verified evidence and testimonials from reputable sources. Seek independent advice from financial professionals or experienced investors. By doing your homework, you can identify potential scams and make informed decisions.

Consider Risk and Return: It is essential to understand that higher returns typically come with higher risks. Investments promising sky-high returns without commensurate risk may be indicators of fraudulent schemes. Assess the risk-reward ratio of any investment opportunity and ensure it aligns with your risk tolerance and long-term financial goals.

Focus on Sustainable Wealth-Building: Sustainable wealth-building strategies emphasize patience, consistency, and a long-term perspective. Avoid chasing short-term gains or succumbing to market fads. Instead, focus on proven investment principles such as diversification, dollar-cost averaging, and disciplined asset allocation. These strategies help you weather market fluctuations and build wealth over time.

Seek Professional Guidance: If you find yourself unsure or overwhelmed by investment options, consider seeking guidance from a qualified financial advisor. A professional advisor can provide personalized advice tailored to your unique financial situation and goals. They can help you navigate the investment landscape, identify suitable opportunities, and avoid common pitfalls.

Patience and Consistency: Building lasting wealth requires patience and consistency. Avoid the temptation to constantly chase the next big thing or jump from one investment to another. Stick to your long-term investment plan and maintain a disciplined approach. Remember that true wealth accumulation is a marathon, not a sprint.

Embrace a Long-Term Perspective: Develop a long-term perspective when it comes to investing. Avoid being swayed by short-term market volatility or short-lived trends. Stay focused on your financial goals and the principles of sustainable wealth-building. By adopting a long-term mindset, you can weather market downturns, take advantage of compounding returns, and build lasting financial security.

Surround Yourself with Like-Minded Individuals: Surrounding

yourself with individuals who share your commitment to sustainable wealth-building can provide support, encouragement, and accountability. Seek out communities, forums, or investment groups where you can connect with like-minded individuals. Engage in discussions, share experiences, and learn from one another.

Practice Emotional Discipline: Emotional discipline is vital in avoiding get-rich-quick schemes. Avoid making impulsive investment decisions based on fear or greed. Emotions can cloud judgment and lead to poor financial choices. Instead, maintain a calm and rational approach to investing, relying on research, analysis, and a long-term perspective.

By being aware of the dangers of get-rich-quick schemes and committing to a patient, consistent, and sustainable approach to wealth-building, you can protect your financial future. Remember that building wealth is a journey that requires time, effort, and informed decision-making.

CHAPTER 12: HUSTLE HARD

In the pursuit of financial freedom and a life of abundance, it is crucial to explore strategies for maximizing your income potential. By proactively seeking opportunities and creating multiple streams of income, you can increase your earning power and create a solid foundation for your financial goals. In this chapter, we will delve into practical points and actionable steps to help you hustle hard and unlock your income potential.

Identify Your Skills and Passions: Start by identifying your unique skills and passions. What are you naturally good at, and what do you enjoy doing? Understanding your strengths and interests will help you align your income-generating activities with your personal preferences and increase the chances of long-term success.

Invest in Continuous Learning: Commit to lifelong learning and personal development. Acquire new knowledge, skills, and certifications that are relevant to your field of interest. Stay updated with industry trends and advancements to remain competitive and expand your income opportunities.

Leverage Your Network: Networking is a powerful tool for unlocking income potential. Build and nurture relationships within your industry and beyond. Attend conferences, seminars, and networking events to connect with like-minded professionals and potential collaborators or clients. Your network can open doors to new opportunities and provide valuable insights and support.

Freelancing and Consulting: Consider freelancing or consulting as a way to monetize your expertise. Offering your services on a freelance basis allows you to leverage your skills and knowledge to generate income independently. Identify market demand for your skills and create a compelling value proposition to attract clients and secure projects.

Side Hustles: Explore side hustles that align with your interests and skills. A side hustle can be an additional source of income and a platform for exploring new passions. Identify opportunities that fit your schedule and can be pursued alongside your primary income source. Launch a small online business, monetize a hobby, or offer specialized services on a part-time basis.

Monetize Your Passion: If you have a passion that can be turned into a profitable venture, consider monetizing it. Whether it's creating and selling artwork, writing a blog, or starting a YouTube channel, find ways to share your passion with others and generate income from it. With dedication and consistency, your passion project can become a sustainable source of income.

Passive Income Streams: Explore opportunities for generating passive income. Passive income refers to earnings that require minimal ongoing effort once set up. Examples include rental properties, dividend stocks, and creating digital products. Research different passive income streams and choose ones that align with your financial goals and risk tolerance.

Develop an Entrepreneurial Mindset: Cultivate an entrepreneurial mindset to identify and seize opportunities. Develop a problem-solving mindset and be proactive in seeking solutions for others. Entrepreneurship allows you to create your own income streams, innovate, and have control over your financial destiny.

Embrace Online Platforms: Leverage the power of online platforms to expand your reach and income potential. Whether it's selling products on e-commerce platforms, offering online courses, or providing remote services, the internet provides numerous opportunities to connect with a global audience and monetize your skills.

Balance Passion and Practicality: When maximizing your income potential, strike a balance between pursuing your passions and considering practicality. While it's important to find joy in your work, be mindful of market demand and income potential. Assess the viability of different income streams and ensure they align with your financial goals.

Track and Optimize: Monitor your income streams and track your financial progress. Regularly evaluate the performance of each income source and identify areas for improvement. Optimize your efforts by focusing on the income streams that generate the highest returns and consider reallocating resources accordingly.

Embrace a Growth Mindset: Adopt a growth mindset and be open to experimentation and adaptation. Embrace challenges as opportunities for growth and view setbacks as learning experiences. Continually assess and refine your income-generating strategies to stay ahead in a rapidly changing world.

By implementing these strategies and embracing the hustle mindset, you can maximize your income potential and create multiple streams of income.

CHAPTER 13: APPRECIATING ASSETS

In this chapter, we will explore the importance of appreciating assets and how they can help you build long-term wealth. By investing in assets that appreciate over time, such as real estate, stocks, and other appreciating investments, you can protect and grow your net worth. Let's dive into practical points to help you make informed decisions about building your wealth through appreciating assets:

Understand Appreciating Assets:

Educate yourself about different types of appreciating assets, including real estate, stocks, bonds, and other investment vehicles.

Research historical trends and performance of various assets to gain insights into their potential for appreciation over time.

Consider consulting with financial advisors or experts who can provide guidance tailored to your specific financial goals and circumstances.

Diversify Your Portfolio:

Spread your investments across a variety of appreciating assets to reduce risk and increase potential returns.

Allocate your assets based on your risk tolerance, investment timeline, and financial objectives.

Regularly review and rebalance your portfolio to ensure it remains aligned with your goals and market conditions.

Real Estate Investments:

Explore real estate opportunities, such as residential or commercial properties, rental properties, or real estate investment trusts (REITs).

Conduct thorough research on the local market, property values, rental demand, and potential for future growth.

Consider factors like location, property condition, and

potential rental income when evaluating real estate investment opportunities.

Stock Market Investments:

Understand the basics of stock market investing, including different investment vehicles like individual stocks, exchange-traded funds (ETFs), or mutual funds.

Conduct thorough research on companies or sectors you are interested in and analyze their financial performance, growth prospects, and market trends.

Consider a long-term investment approach to benefit from compounding growth and ride out short-term market fluctuations.

Other Appreciating Investments:

Explore other investment opportunities like bonds, commodities, or alternative investments such as art, collectibles, or cryptocurrencies.

Evaluate the risks and potential returns associated with each investment class, considering your risk tolerance and investment strategy.

Seek expert advice or specialized knowledge before investing in complex or less traditional assets.

Protect and Grow Your Net Worth:

Regularly review and assess the performance of your appreciating assets to ensure they align with your financial goals.

Implement risk management strategies such as insurance, diversification, and asset protection to safeguard your wealth.

Consider tax-efficient investment strategies to maximize your returns and minimize tax liabilities.

Continual Learning and Adjustment:

Stay informed about changes in the investment landscape, market trends, and regulatory updates that may affect your assets.

Continue to educate yourself about investment strategies, asset classes, and financial management principles.

Be open to adjusting your investment approach based on changing market conditions or shifts in your personal financial situation.

Seek Professional Advice:

Consider working with a financial advisor or investment professional who can provide personalized guidance based on your specific goals and risk tolerance.

Look for professionals who have a fiduciary duty to act in your best interest and have a track record of success in wealth management.

Remember, building long-term wealth through appreciating assets requires patience, discipline, and a long-term perspective. Stay informed, diversify your portfolio, and regularly assess your investments. By appreciating the value of assets, you can protect and grow your net worth, providing a solid foundation for your financial future.

CHAPTER 14: PROTECTING YOUR KINGDOM: SAFEGUARDING YOUR ASSETS

As you progress on your journey to financial freedom, it becomes crucial to protect the assets you've worked so hard to accumulate. In this chapter, we will explore practical strategies for diversifying income streams, managing risks, and making informed life decisions with financial prudence. By safeguarding your assets, you can create a solid foundation for long-term financial security and peace of mind.

Diversifying Income Streams: Relying on a single source of income can leave you vulnerable to financial instability. Consider diversifying your income streams to increase financial resilience. Explore opportunities for creating multiple streams of income, such as starting a side business, investing in dividend-paying stocks, or generating passive income through rental properties. Diversification not only provides additional financial security but also opens up new avenues for wealth accumulation.

Building an Emergency Fund: Life is unpredictable, and unexpected expenses can quickly derail your financial progress. Establishing an emergency fund is crucial to protect your assets and maintain stability. Aim to save at least three to six months' worth of living expenses in a separate, easily accessible account. This fund will serve as a safety net during challenging times, helping you avoid debt and providing peace of mind.

Managing Insurance: Insurance is a vital tool for protecting your assets and managing risks. Assess your insurance needs and ensure adequate coverage for your health, property, and valuable possessions. Evaluate your insurance policies regularly to ensure they align with your current circumstances and adequately protect your assets. Consider working with a reputable insurance agent or financial advisor to identify any gaps in coverage and make informed decisions.

Estate Planning: Planning for the future is essential to protect your assets and ensure a smooth transfer of wealth. Consult an estate planning attorney to create a comprehensive plan that includes a will, power of attorney, healthcare directive, and, if applicable, a trust. Review and update your estate plan regularly to reflect any changes in your financial situation, family dynamics, or personal preferences.

Minimizing Debt: High levels of debt can compromise your financial security and limit your options. Prioritize reducing and eliminating debt to safeguard your assets. Focus on paying off high-interest debt first, such as credit cards or personal loans. Explore strategies such as debt consolidation, negotiating lower interest rates, or seeking professional assistance if needed. By minimizing debt, you free up resources to invest, save, and protect your assets.

Evaluating Life Decisions: When making significant life decisions, such as career changes, starting a business, or relocating, consider the potential impact on your financial well-being. Evaluate the risks and rewards associated with each decision and weigh them against your long-term financial goals. Seek advice from trusted mentors, financial advisors, or life coaches who can provide guidance based on their expertise and experience.

Regularly Reviewing Investments: Stay vigilant about monitoring and reviewing your investment portfolio. Periodically assess the performance, risk profile, and alignment with your financial goals. Adjust your investment strategy as necessary to optimize returns and manage risks effectively. Stay informed about market trends and changes that may affect your investments, and consider consulting a financial advisor for guidance on rebalancing or diversifying your portfolio.

Continual Learning and Adaptation: The financial landscape is ever-evolving, and it's crucial to stay informed and adapt to changing circumstances. Invest in your financial education by reading books, attending seminars, and following reputable financial news sources. Enhance your understanding of investment strategies, risk management techniques, and emerging trends. By staying informed and adaptable, you can protect your assets and make informed financial decisions.

Regularly Updating Legal Documents: Life changes, and so should your legal documents. Review and update your will, insurance policies, and beneficiary designations after major life events such as marriage, divorce, the birth of a child, or the acquisition of significant assets. Keeping your legal documents up to date ensures that your assets are distributed according to your wishes and protects your loved ones.

Seeking Professional Guidance: When navigating complex financial matters, don't hesitate to seek professional advice. Engage with reputable financial advisors, attorneys, or accountants who can provide guidance tailored to your specific situation. Working with professionals ensures that you make informed decisions, manage risks effectively, and safeguard your assets.

By implementing these strategies for protecting your kingdom, you fortify your financial position and create a solid base for long-term security.

CHAPTER 15: THE MINIMALIST MINDSET

In a world that often equates success with material possessions, it's essential to redefine our understanding of fulfillment and prioritize experiences over things. The minimalist mindset empowers us to simplify our lives, cultivate personal growth, and discover true freedom and fulfillment. In this chapter, we will explore practical strategies for embracing a minimalist mindset and redefining success beyond material possessions.

Prioritizing Experiences: Shift your focus from acquiring material possessions to accumulating meaningful experiences. Allocate your time, energy, and resources toward activities that align with your values and bring you joy and fulfillment. Engage in hobbies, travel, volunteer work, or pursue personal development opportunities. By prioritizing experiences, you enrich your life with memories and personal growth rather than relying on material possessions for happiness.

Simplifying Your Life: Embrace simplicity by decluttering your physical and mental space. Evaluate your belongings and let go of items that no longer serve a purpose or bring you joy. Adopt a minimalist approach to material possessions by practicing mindful consumption and avoiding unnecessary purchases. Streamline your daily routines, commitments, and obligations to create more time and space for the things that truly matter.

Defining Success on Your Own Terms: Challenge society's definition of success and establish your own parameters for fulfillment. Reflect on what truly brings you happiness and a sense of achievement. Is it the accumulation of wealth and possessions, or is it the pursuit of personal growth, meaningful relationships, and a sense of purpose? Align your goals and aspirations with your core values to create a life that is authentically yours.

Cultivating Gratitude: Develop a habit of gratitude to appreciate the abundance in your life. Focus on the present moment and the positive aspects of your experiences, relationships, and personal growth. Practice gratitude exercises such as keeping a gratitude journal or expressing appreciation to others. By cultivating gratitude, you shift your mindset toward abundance and contentment, reducing the desire for excessive material possessions.

Intentional Spending: Adopt a mindful approach to spending by aligning your purchases with your values and long-term goals. Before making a purchase, ask yourself if it contributes to your well-being, personal growth, or experiences. Avoid impulsive buying and consider the long-term impact of your purchases on your financial and mental well-being. By practicing intentional spending, you redirect your resources toward what truly matters to you.

Investing in Relationships: Place a greater emphasis on nurturing and investing in meaningful relationships. Allocate time and energy to cultivate strong connections with family, friends, and your community. Engage in deep conversations, shared experiences, and acts of kindness. Meaningful relationships provide a sense of fulfillment and support that material possessions cannot replicate.

Seeking Inner Fulfillment: Look inward for fulfillment by focusing on personal growth and self-awareness. Engage in practices such as meditation, mindfulness, or journaling to develop a deeper understanding of yourself and your values. Explore your passions, talents, and areas of personal development. By seeking inner fulfillment, you rely less on external validations and material possessions for happiness.

Living with Intention: Make conscious choices that align with your values and goals. Approach each day with purpose and intention, considering the impact of your actions on yourself and others. Set meaningful goals that encompass personal growth, relationships, and experiences rather than solely focusing on material achievements. By living with intention, you create a life that reflects your values and brings you true fulfillment.

Embracing Minimalist Practices: Explore minimalist practices that resonate with you and incorporate them into your daily life. This could include adopting a capsule wardrobe, simplifying your home environment, or reducing digital distractions. Experiment with different practices and find what works best for you in simplifying and decluttering various aspects of your life.

Letting Go of Comparison: Release the need to compare yourself to others based on material possessions or external achievements. Remember that everyone's journey is unique, and true fulfillment comes from within. Celebrate your own progress, growth, and experiences rather than constantly measuring yourself against societal standards. Focus on your personal journey and embrace the path that brings you the most joy and fulfillment.

By embracing a minimalist mindset and prioritizing experiences over material possessions, you open the door to a life of greater freedom, fulfillment, and authenticity.

CHAPTER 16: REDEFINING RETIREMENT

Retirement, traditionally seen as a phase of life marked by leisure and relaxation, is undergoing a transformation. In today's world, retirement is no longer solely about withdrawing from work but rather redefining it as a time to pursue meaningful endeavors and find fulfillment. In this chapter, we will explore how you can redefine retirement to create a life of purpose, invest in your health for long-term freedom, and continue your journey of personal growth.

Rethinking Traditional Notions of Retirement: Challenge the conventional idea of retirement as an endpoint or withdrawal from work. Instead, view it as a new chapter that allows you to explore your passions, engage in purposeful work, and contribute to society in meaningful ways. Embrace the opportunity to design a retirement lifestyle that aligns with your values, interests, and aspirations.

Finding Fulfillment and Purpose in Your Work: Retirement doesn't mean completely abandoning work; it means transitioning to work that brings you joy and fulfillment. Identify your passions and explore how you can channel them into meaningful projects, consulting work, or volunteering opportunities. Seek work that aligns with your values and allows you to make a positive impact on others.

Pursuing a Balanced Lifestyle: As you redefine retirement, strive for a balanced lifestyle that includes leisure, personal growth, and contribution. Allocate time for relaxation, hobbies, travel, and spending quality time with loved ones. Engage in activities that promote mental, physical, and emotional well-being, such as exercise, learning, and self-care practices.

Investing in Health for Long-Term Freedom: Retirement offers an opportunity to invest in your health and well-being. Prioritize healthy habits, including regular exercise, a balanced diet, and sufficient rest. Consider engaging in activities that promote mental acuity, such as puzzles, reading, or learning new skills. By investing in your health, you increase your longevity and ensure a fulfilling retirement.

Embracing Continuous Learning: Retirement is an ideal time to pursue new knowledge and skills. Engage in lifelong learning through courses, workshops, or online platforms. Explore subjects that interest you and challenge yourself intellectually. Continuous learning keeps your mind sharp, expands your horizons, and opens up new possibilities for personal growth and contribution.

Pursuing Passion Projects and New Ventures: Use your retirement as an opportunity to pursue passion projects or start new ventures. Identify areas of interest that have always intrigued you but were previously put on hold due to career obligations. Whether it's starting a small business, writing a book, or engaging in creative endeavors, let your retirement be a time for pursuing your dreams and passions.

Fostering a Sense of Purpose and Fulfillment: Cultivate a strong sense of purpose in your retirement. Reflect on what matters most to you and the legacy you want to leave behind. Consider how you can make a positive impact on others and contribute to causes that align with your values. By finding and pursuing a sense of purpose, you infuse your retirement years with meaning and fulfillment.

Embracing New Challenges and Growth Opportunities: Don't shy away from challenges and growth opportunities in retirement. Step out of your comfort zone and embrace new experiences that push you to learn, adapt, and grow. Travel to new places, engage in cultural exchanges, and embrace diverse perspectives. Continually seek ways to expand your horizons and foster personal growth.

Building and Nurturing Relationships: Prioritize relationships and social connections in your retirement. Invest time and effort in maintaining and nurturing meaningful relationships with family, friends, and community. Engage in activities that foster connection and provide opportunities for shared experiences. Strong relationships enhance your well-being and contribute to a fulfilling retirement.

Embracing Flexibility: In retirement, embrace the freedom to design your own schedule and make adjustments as needed. Embrace the flexibility to pursue new interests, take breaks when necessary, and adapt your plans to changing circumstances. Enjoy the freedom to prioritize your well-being and happiness without the constraints of traditional work obligations.

As you redefine retirement, remember that it is a personal journey unique to you. Embrace the opportunity to create a life of purpose, continue your personal growth, and contribute to the world in meaningful ways.

CHAPTER 17: CULTIVATING A LIFELONG JOURNEY

In your journey as a nomadic black sheep, it is essential to embrace continuous learning and personal growth. One powerful way to do this is through engaging in passion projects and pursuing new ventures that align with your interests and values. In this chapter, we will explore the power of projects and how they can fuel your sense of purpose, provide opportunities for personal development, and foster a deep sense of fulfillment.

Embracing Continuous Learning: As a digital nomdic, your curiosity and thirst for knowledge are valuable assets. Continuously seek opportunities to expand your knowledge and skills. Take courses, attend workshops, or participate in online learning platforms to deepen your understanding of areas that interest you. Cultivate a growth mindset that embraces learning as a lifelong journey.

Pursuing Passion Projects: Passion projects are endeavors driven by your interests, values, and creative expression. They provide a space for you to explore your passions and turn ideas into reality. Identify areas that ignite your enthusiasm and develop projects that allow you to express yourself authentically. Whether it's writing a book, starting a podcast, or launching a social impact initiative, pursue projects that align with your vision and purpose.

Setting Goals and Milestones: Define clear goals and milestones for your passion projects. Break them down into actionable steps and create a timeline to keep yourself accountable. Setting goals provides structure and direction, helping you stay focused and motivated as you work towards completing your projects. Celebrate milestones along the way to acknowledge your progress and keep your momentum going.

Embracing the Process: It's important to remember that the

journey itself holds value. Embrace the process of working on your passion projects, as it provides an opportunity for personal growth, learning, and self-discovery. Stay open to new ideas and perspectives, and be willing to adapt your approach as needed. View challenges and setbacks as valuable learning experiences that contribute to your development.

Collaborating and Networking: Engage with like-minded individuals who share similar interests and values. Collaborate with others who can bring different perspectives and skills to your projects. Networking within your niche or industry can open doors to new opportunities, collaborations, and support systems. Building meaningful connections can enhance your project outcomes and create lasting relationships.

Managing Time and Resources: Effective project management is crucial for success. Break down your projects into manageable tasks and allocate dedicated time to work on them consistently. Prioritize your activities and manage your time efficiently, ensuring a healthy balance between your passion projects and other aspects of your life. Maximize your resources by leveraging tools, technologies, and supportive networks to optimize your project outcomes.

Fostering a Sense of Purpose: Passion projects have the potential to ignite a deep sense of purpose within you. Align your projects with your values and vision, infusing them with a greater meaning and impact. Reflect on how your projects contribute to your personal growth, the well-being of others, or a cause you care about. By connecting your passion projects to a sense of purpose, you enhance their significance and create a lasting impact.

Embracing Adaptability and Flexibility: Projects may evolve and take unexpected turns along the way. Embrace adaptability and flexibility as essential skills to navigate the dynamic nature of your projects. Be open to new ideas, feedback, and opportunities that arise during the project's journey. Stay nimble and willing to adjust your plans when necessary, allowing your projects to grow and evolve organically.

Celebrating Achievements and Lessons Learned: Throughout your project journey, celebrate achievements and milestones, no matter how big or small. Recognize and acknowledge your progress, growth, and the impact you've made. Equally important is reflecting on lessons learned from challenges and setbacks. Embrace a mindset of continuous improvement and apply the insights gained from each project to future endeavors.

Balancing Projects and Well-being: While projects are exciting and fulfilling, it's essential to maintain a healthy balance. Prioritize self-care, relaxation, and well-being alongside your project work. Set boundaries, manage your energy levels, and engage in activities that rejuvenate you. By prioritizing your well-being, you can sustain your passion and commitment to your projects in the long run.

Remember, the power of projects lies in their ability to fuel your sense of purpose, provide avenues for personal growth, and contribute to your overall fulfillment. By embracing continuous learning, pursuing passion projects, and cultivating a lifelong journey, you enhance your maverick lifestyle and create a lasting impact.

CHAPTER 18: FINANCIAL FREEDOM

Financial freedom is the cornerstone of your journey as a maverick against society. It is the key that unlocks the doors to a life of flexibility, autonomy, and abundance. In this chapter, we will explore the concept of financial freedom and guide you through the process of discovering your personal number— the amount needed for you to achieve financial independence. Additionally, we will provide strategies for achieving financial freedom sooner and maximizing your resources for long-term security.

Clarifying Your Financial Goals: Begin by clarifying your financial goals and envisioning the life you desire. Reflect on the lifestyle you want to live, your desired level of financial security, and the experiences you wish to have. Define what financial freedom means to you personally, as it may vary from one individual to another.

Calculating Your Financial Independence Number: Your financial independence number is the amount of money required to cover your living expenses and sustain your desired lifestyle without relying on traditional employment income. To calculate this number, assess your current expenses and determine the annual amount needed to sustain your desired lifestyle. Consider factors such as housing, transportation, healthcare, food, travel, and any other significant expenses.

Strategies for Achieving Financial Freedom Sooner: Once you have determined your financial independence number, it's time to strategize how to achieve it sooner. Consider the following practical points:

Increase your income: Explore opportunities to increase your monthly income. This could involve negotiating a raise, starting a side business, or developing additional income streams aligned with your skills and passions.

Reduce expenses: Evaluate your current expenses and identify areas where you can cut back. Optimize your spending habits by distinguishing between needs and wants, and prioritize your financial goals.

Save and invest wisely: Develop a disciplined savings plan and allocate a portion of your income towards investments. Explore different investment vehicles such as stocks, bonds, real estate, or business ventures. Diversify your portfolio to mitigate risk and maximize returns.

Automate your finances: Set up automatic transfers to your savings and investment accounts to ensure consistent contributions. Automating your finances eliminates the temptation to spend impulsively and ensures that you are consistently saving and investing towards your financial goals.

Seek financial guidance: Consider consulting with a financial advisor or coach who specializes in helping individuals achieve financial independence. They can provide personalized guidance based on your unique circumstances and help you make informed decisions.

Maximizing Your Resources for Long-Term Security: Building long-term financial security requires strategic planning and utilizing various resources. Consider the following practical points:

Continuously educate yourself: Stay informed about personal finance and investment strategies. Educate yourself on different financial vehicles, tax strategies, and wealth-building techniques. Empower yourself with knowledge and make informed decisions about your financial future.

Leverage technology: Utilize financial apps and online tools to track your expenses, manage your budget, and monitor your investments. Technology can simplify the process of managing your finances, providing you with real-time information and insights to make better financial decisions.

Protect your assets: Safeguard your assets by ensuring you have appropriate insurance coverage for your health, home, business, and other significant assets. Regularly review your insurance policies to ensure they align with your current needs and provide adequate protection.

Continually reassess and adjust: Life circumstances change, and your financial plan should adapt accordingly. Regularly reassess your goals, income, expenses, and investments. Make adjustments as needed to stay on track and align your financial strategies with your evolving aspirations.

Foster a growth mindset: Cultivate a mindset of abundance and wealth consciousness. Believe in your ability to achieve financial freedom and attract opportunities for growth. Adopting a positive mindset will support your long-term financial success.

By discovering your personal financial independence number and implementing strategies to achieve it, you pave the way towards a life of financial freedom. Remember that financial independence is not solely about accumulating wealth but also about aligning your financial resources with your desired lifestyle and values.

CHAPTER 19: SUSTAINING FREEDOM

Congratulations! You have embarked on a journey of financial freedom and personal liberation in your heist against society. In this chapter, we will explore how to sustain the freedom you have achieved and find balance and fulfillment in your newfound lifestyle. Adapting to the challenges and joys of financial freedom requires conscious effort and a holistic approach that encompasses managing your time, nurturing relationships, and fostering personal growth. Let's delve into practical points that will help you sustain your freedom and thrive in your new life.

Time Management for Fulfillment:

Identify your priorities: Clarify your values and define what truly matters to you. Use these priorities as a guide when making decisions about how to allocate your time.
Set boundaries: Establish boundaries to protect your time and energy. Learn to say no to commitments that don't align with your priorities and goals.

Create a schedule that works for you: Design a schedule that reflects your preferred working style and optimal productivity. Experiment with different routines and find what works best for you.

Embrace flexibility: While structure is essential, embrace the flexibility that comes with your new lifestyle. Allow for spontaneity and adaptability in your daily routine.
Nurturing Relationships:

Cultivate a support network: Surround yourself with like-minded individuals who understand and support your journey. Connect with fellow digital nomads, join communities, and foster meaningful relationships.

Communicate openly: Effective communication is crucial in

maintaining healthy relationships. Be open, honest, and transparent about your lifestyle choices and aspirations with your loved ones.

Prioritize quality time: Dedicate quality time to the people who matter most to you. Build strong connections and create lasting memories through shared experiences.

Embrace technology: Leverage technology to stay connected with friends and family, no matter where you are. Utilize video calls, messaging apps, and social media platforms to bridge the distance.

Personal Growth and Fulfillment:

Continue learning: Embrace a mindset of continuous learning and personal growth. Engage in professional development, explore new interests, and expand your knowledge and skills.

Pursue passion projects: Dedicate time to pursuing passion projects and ventures that align with your values and interests. These projects can provide a sense of purpose and fulfillment beyond financial success.

Practice self-care: Prioritize self-care to maintain your physical, mental, and emotional well-being. Incorporate activities such as exercise, meditation, journaling, and hobbies into your routine.

Embrace gratitude: Cultivate a practice of gratitude to enhance your overall well-being. Regularly acknowledge and appreciate the abundance in your life.
Finding Balance:

Assess and adjust: Regularly assess your lifestyle and make adjustments as needed. Reflect on what is working well and what needs improvement. Aim for a balance that aligns with your values and brings you joy.

Embrace downtime: Allow yourself to rest and recharge. Schedule regular breaks and periods of relaxation to prevent burnout and maintain your energy levels.

Emphasize experiences over possessions: As a nomadic black sheep, prioritize experiences and personal growth over material possessions. Seek fulfillment through new adventures, connections, and learning opportunities.

Remember, sustaining freedom is an ongoing process that requires self-awareness, adaptability, and conscious choices. Regularly evaluate your progress, celebrate your successes, and make necessary adjustments to align with your evolving aspirations. By nurturing your relationships, managing your time effectively, fostering personal growth, and finding balance, you will thrive in your new life of audacity and abundance.

CHAPTER 20: THE HEIST AGAINST SOCIETY

This chapter marks the beginning of a new phase in your life—the moment when you consolidate your knowledge, embrace your maverick spirit, and take action towards financial freedom and personal liberation. It's time to write your own rules for a life of audacity and abundance. Let's explore practical points to guide you on this transformative journey.

Reflect on Your Journey:

Take time to reflect on how far you've come. Celebrate your achievements, both big and small, and acknowledge the growth and progress you've experienced throughout this process.
Consider the lessons you've learned and the insights you've gained. Reflect on the challenges you've overcome and the skills you've developed along the way.
Identify the values and principles that have guided you thus far. Use these as a foundation for creating a vision for your future.
Embrace Your Maverick Spirit:

Embrace your unique qualities, strengths, and passions. Recognize that it is your individuality that sets you apart and fuels your potential for greatness.
Challenge the status quo and conventional wisdom. Embrace audacity, boldness, and cheekiness as you carve your own path in life and business.
Cultivate a mindset of limitless possibilities. Believe in your ability to create meaningful change and contribute to a better world.
Define Your Personal Definition of Success:

Reflect on what success truly means to you. Is it financial freedom, creative fulfillment, making a positive impact, or a combination of various aspects of your life?

Identify your core values and align your goals and actions with them. Let your personal definition of success be a compass that guides your decision-making process.

Remember that success is a journey, not a destination. Embrace the process and celebrate the small wins along the way.

Take Action:

Develop an action plan to bring your vision to life. Break it down into smaller, manageable steps and set realistic timelines for each milestone.

Prioritize your actions based on their impact and alignment with your goals. Focus on tasks that will move you closer to your desired outcomes.

Hold yourself accountable. Regularly review your progress, adjust your approach if necessary, and stay committed to taking consistent action.

Surround Yourself with Supportive Networks:

Seek out communities and networks that align with your values and aspirations. Connect with like-minded individuals who can offer support, guidance, and inspiration.

Build relationships with mentors and role models who have achieved what you aspire to accomplish. Learn from their experiences and leverage their knowledge to accelerate your own growth.

Engage in collaboration and partnership opportunities. Surround yourself with a team of individuals who complement your skills and share your vision.

Embrace Continuous Learning and Growth:

Never stop learning. Stay curious and open to new ideas, perspectives, and experiences. Seek out opportunities for personal and professional development.

Invest in your skills and knowledge. Identify areas where you can enhance your expertise and commit to ongoing education and self-improvement.

Embrace failure as a stepping stone to success. Learn from your mistakes, adjust your approach, and use setbacks as opportunities for growth and resilience.
Live with Intention and Gratitude:

Live each day with purpose and intention. Align your actions with your values and goals, and be mindful of how you spend your time and energy.

Practice gratitude daily. Cultivate an attitude of appreciation for the present moment, the opportunities you have, and the people who support you.

Be kind to yourself. Celebrate your achievements, practice self-care, and prioritize your well-being throughout this journey.

As you embark on this new phase of your life, remember that the heist against society is not about rebellion for the sake of rebellion, but about creating a life that is true to who you are and aligns with your values and aspirations. Embrace the freedom and responsibility that comes with writing your own rules, and let audacity and abundance guide your actions.

Now, go forth and create the life of your dreams—one that is bold, purposeful, and aligned with your authentic self. Your journey begins now.